MW00576905

THE CEO ROLE
UNDER POLICY
GOVERNANCE

John Carver and
Miriam Mayhew Carver

JOSSEY-BASS
A Wiley Company
www.josseybass.com

Published by

JOSSEY-BASS
A Wiley Company
989 Market Street
San Francisco, CA 94103-1741

www.josseybass.com

Jossey-Bass books and products are available through most bookstores. To contact Jossey-Bass directly, call (888) 378-2537, fax to (800) 605-2665, or visit our website at www.josseybass.com.

Substantial discounts on bulk quantities of Jossey-Bass books are available to corporations, professional associations, and other organizations. For details and discount information, contact the special sales department at Jossey-Bass.

We at Jossey-Bass strive to use the most environmentally sensitive paper stocks available to us. Our publications are printed on acid-free recycled stock whenever possible, and our paper always meets or exceeds minimum GPO and EPA requirements.

Wiley also publishes its books in a variety of electronic formats. Some content that appears in print may not be available in electronic books.

Policy Governance® is a registered service mark of John Carver.

Library of Congress Cataloging-in-Publication Data

Carver, John.
    The CEO role under policy governance / by John Carver and
Miriam Mayhew Carver. — 1st ed.
        p. cm. — (CarverGuide ; 12)
      ISBN 0–7879–1084–8 (pbk.)
      1. Chief executive officers. 2. Corporate governance.
   3. Directors of corporations. I. Carver, Miriam Mayhew. II. Title.
III. Series: Carver, John. The CarverGuide series on effective board
governance ; 12.
    HD38.C373   1997
    658.4'2—dc21   97-21105

PB Printing   10 9 8 7 6 5   FIRST EDITION

CARVERGUIDE

Generally, we write to boards of directors about Policy Governance because the model is designed for boards, not for CEOs. The renewal and maintenance of governance capability are the responsibilities of boards, not—as many boards are wont to construe it—of CEOs. It should not be up to CEOs to make sure their bosses conduct themselves responsibly. But, as we know, boards frequently send a confusing message to their CEO: "You work for us. Now tell us what to do!" They act as if the CEO is more responsible for the board's behavior than its own members are, and you, as the CEO, often believe it.

We have written this CarverGuide to help you, the CEO, work better with your board. As your board is defining its role in the Policy Governance model and becoming a strategic leader, you will be defining your role as CEO. Implementing the model in your organization requires that both you and the board understand and carry out the new roles required by the model.

So, this CarverGuide looks at Policy Governance from your perspective. We begin with a section that looks at your role as CEO in the more traditional models of board governance. In the next section, we contrast the "old way" of thinking about the CEO to the "new way" through Policy Governance. The next two sections cover how your board relates to you in traditional models versus how they should relate to you under Policy Governance. A crucial part of your relationship is the trust between you and your board because this is often seen as the all-important "glue" that keeps boards and CEOs working together happily ever after. So we spend some time on this topic. Last, since many CEOs are faced with the challenge of help-ing their boards conduct their business using the Policy Gover-nance model, we also provide you with some tips to help your board keep from slipping back to the old ways of doing things.

The CEO's Role in Traditional Governance

As CEO, you may have one of many titles. You may be the execu-tive director, superintendent, executive vice president, general man-ager, chief staff officer, county administrator, or director-general. Your title, however, means nothing in itself.

You have a job regardless of your title, and this job can be described in various ways. Traditional job descriptions tend to focus on the activities you are expected to perform. For instance, yours might read as follows:

- Administer the agency
- Hire and supervise staff
- Evaluate staff and programs
- Write budgets and program plans
- Represent the agency to local officials
- Write grant applications
- Oversee care of the property
- Submit financial reports

We don't recommend this method of describing a CEO role. Listing tasks actually misses the point of what a CEO job is for. Your board needs you, but not to stay busy at various tasks, even seem-ingly necessary ones. The board needs you to make sure that the total operational organization is working in a way that is sure to make the organization meet the board's expectations.

Boards focus on CEO activities when describing the CEO role because they have traditionally seen their own role as needing to delve into internal arrangements such as organization charts and departmental structures. Boards even fall into delegating directly to these sub-CEO structural components (for example, giving a certain job to the public relations department or charging the accounting department with a task). Further, boards like to judge the performance of sub-CEO personnel or departments. This is because boards see no alternative, if they are to remain accountable for their organizations, but to involve themselves directly in many disparate parts of operations. They fail, of course, to see that their control is of a very uneven and incomplete nature when using this method.

The result is that the CEO job is almost impossible to define. Boards are unable to clearly delegate; CEOs are unable to distinguish their jobs from the jobs of the board or board committees; and CEOs grapple with a job in which they are seemingly going to be held accountable for matters over which they were given no authority. Worse, any system or method of job definition that develops is dependent solely on the personalities of the incumbent players, CEO, chair, board, and so forth. Obviously, no system that is this personality-dependent can be considered a system with any design integrity.

It is usual to see traditional boards give disproportionate attention to items of trivial scope or import compared with matters of greater scope or import. Questions of purpose go unresolved while boards conscientiously grapple with small details. And CEOs find their board consistently reacting to staff initiatives rather than being proactive. Proposals for staff action and recommendations for board action so often come from staff that some boards would cease to function if called upon to create their own agendas. It may be possible, therefore, to define the role of the CEO under traditional governance as a role wherein all decisions are seen by the board as suspect (in need of line-by-line scrutiny) but also wherein the board is dependent on the CEO to stage-manage the board itself. The CEO role is both difficult and dangerous!

The CEO's Role in Policy Governance

What does it take to be a real CEO? The answer lies in two features of the role: authority and accountability. Whether your staff is few or many, an uncountable number of their combined actions must come together well in order to produce a successful organization.

In a way, your job is like the narrow part of a venturi or the constricted waist of an egg timer. Above the CEO is a group of people, albeit acting as one, that determines expectations for the organization's production and character. Below the CEO is a group of people, divided by type of labor, that pursues the attainment of those expectations. You are normally the only point in the entire chain of decision making where the "flow" of authority downward and accountability upward go through a single human being. You are ordinarily the only person who works for a group and over a group.

The board, of course, must be responsible for "acting as one," and the CEO must be responsible for the divisions of staff labor intended to produce the desired outcomes. In another sense, while the board has its own "servant-leader"—the chairperson—to assist it in acting properly as one, the board chooses a CEO to worry about all the components of production. The chairperson, therefore, leads the board at the behest of the board; the CEO leads the staff. It is important for you to keep that straight, even though there are ample opportunities to confound these roles.

There can be no CEO job until the board has defined it, as the CEO works for the board and must ensure that the organization meets the board's expectations. Until the board has stated its expectations, the CEO has received no delegation. Indeed, delegation can be seen as the central problem of a governing board. The board is ultimately accountable for an organization it does not see that carries out a multitude of tasks it does not understand. It must therefore charge its CEO with a job that is clear and that carries an unambiguous authority to make decisions. For maximum board and CEO accountability (and peace of mind), it is very important to describe the board and CEO functions as simply as possible.

The board must be clear about its communication to the CEO. It must have rules about (1) just what constitutes a formal board-to-CEO communication and (2) what that communication must contain. It must also deal with (3) the question of who has the right to interpret board communications. In Policy Governance, the CEO's only responsibility is to the board, not to officers of the board or to board committees or to board members as individuals. So, (1) a formal board-to-CEO communication is a policy that has been passed by the board in a properly constituted board meeting; (2) the communication must contain only prescriptions of organizational achievements (ends policies) or proscriptions of unacceptable organizational means (executive limitations policies), both policy types framed at broad levels. To enable a powerful management, (3) the board must give the CEO authority to interpret ends and executive limitations policies. It can do so safely by defining these policies in increasingly narrower terms until it has reached the level of detail where it feels comfortable allowing the CEO to interpret its words.

As CEO, therefore, you are accountable to the board not simply for your own tasks but for the success of the entire organization. Being held accountable to the board for organization performance is a distinct characteristic of the CEO function. From the board's point of view, the important lesson is that the board's relationship with the CEO must be formed around the accountability of the position, not the position's individual tasks, which can vary from CEO to CEO. In other words, it need be none of the board's concern just what hands-on job responsibilities the CEO chooses to retain (that is, not to delegate). The board's concern is confined to the total organizational performance for which it holds the CEO accountable. This all may seem straightforward, but let's consider the implications.

- You are the only employee of the board. All other staff are your employees. If something goes wrong in the organization (that is, there is a failure in producing ends or a violation of the board's executive limitations), there is only one person at whom the board can point its finger. The board has no official connection with staff members except at the CEO's behest.

- The CEO's own personal work need not be a board concern. You are accountable for the entire organization's working up to expectations. Your personal work is immaterial to the board. Your personal job description (as separate from what you have delegated to staff members) is not for the board to decide and certainly not for the board to use in evaluating your performance.

- Board members and the CEO are colleagues. Your relationship with any individual board member is collegial, not hierarchical. Since you are accountable only to the full board, and since no board member has authority individually, the CEO and board members are equals. You are definitely related by hierarchy to the board as a body, however.

Your job, basically, is to work whatever magic it takes to ensure an acceptable amount, type, and targeting of benefits in prudent and ethical ways. Some boards are reluctant to empower the CEO to this extent. Their reasons vary from being unwilling to let go of the strings on decision making to being unwilling to burden CEO and staff with such momentous decisions. But by delegating less authority, the board must constantly forsake strategic leadership to make tactical decisions.

Leadership is being cheated in either case. Perhaps having greater executive authority puts an additional burden on you, but we doubt it. In most cases, you will work no more in making decisions than you already do in *almost* making decisions, such as in writing recommendations or providing support to board committees.

Thus, a summary of your job responsibilities would be as follows:

The chief executive officer is accountable to the board of directors for the organization's (1) achievement of ends policies and (2) non-violation of executive limitations policies.

This is the long and the short of the job. The CEO function neither takes over board prerogatives nor stands meekly aside while the board does staff work. It is a position that is as invested in having a strong board as in having a free hand. It is a function that, being strong, can afford to bid both board and staff to grow.

The Board-CEO Relationship in Traditional Governance

Having often failed to define your reporting relationship cleanly, and having delegated incomplete or unclear expectations and decision-making authority, a traditional board has little alternative but to state your job description in terms of the tasks you personally are expected to perform, including, often, the activities of setting the board agenda, developing the board, and taking responsibility for board actions (or nonactions). What the board does versus what you do, as CEO, becomes muddy in traditional governance. This is why conflict so often occurs in relationships between CEOs and their boards.

Without a clear difference in job contributions, the board becomes a part-time staff, one step removed from the action. It is not unusual for a board to see its job as "stacked" on top of staff jobs. No wonder boards have problems distinguishing their positions from those of their chief executives.

One of the key ways that CEO-board relationships run afoul is when boards make staff-level decisions while CEOs make board-level decisions. Boards make staff decisions through any number of single incursions: a motion to hire someone, a motion to award the painting contract to a certain contractor, a motion to change a certain personnel rule, a motion to switch $300 from one budget line item to another, and so on, ad nauseam.

For as long as anyone can remember, this "approval syndrome" found in traditional governance has been the main tool boards use to monitor staff intentions. In order to be sure things are going acceptably, boards demand approval authority over all manner of internal practices. Personnel policies, budgets, program plans, compensation schedules, and staff promotions are among the familiar actions and documents that boards approve. The board becomes the "watchdog" of the organization by becoming heavily involved in administration. Proper governance as well as proper management suffers.

Boards also intrude into management by trying to help or advise staff in operational areas. Whether given by individuals, committees, or the whole board, advice to staff from the governors becomes confused with direction. When this happens, you are forced to exercise your diplomacy skills to maintain social graces while watching the board's delegation to you, and yours to your staff, becoming more and more muddled. Your staff become confused about to whom they report. Is it their supervisor, or the committee, or the advice-giving board member, or the chair? Your ability to run the operational organization is severely compromised.

Conversely, the expectations that you will assume governance responsibility abound in traditional governance. Boards often wait for your recommendations before moving. Some even believe that to move without the CEO's recommendation is foolhardy. This is often illustrated by how board meeting agendas are set. It is common for boards to defer to their CEOs on agenda sequence and content. They become so dependent on their CEO for agenda preparation that they would be adrift without guidance. As long as boards are only dealing with staff-level material, their instincts are correct.

The problem is circular. Boards are trapped in staff-level issues and, therefore, need staff input as to what those issues are. Staff is called upon to generate board agendas and, therefore, board agendas are composed chiefly of staff-level issues.

But if we remove all staff issues from the board agenda and have only those that truly belong to the board, the scenario changes significantly. Now the same behavior is revealed to be the ostensible leader's waiting for its CEO to tell it what to do next. What the CEO wants the board to do may be of interest and even of some legitimate influence, but it is surely not the driving force of good governance.

Traditional models, then, confound two errors. First, boards deal so predominantly with low-level issues that the executive's not having a controlling influence would be foolish. Second, boards often avoid confronting genuine governance decisions by falling back on executive recommendations. Your board's asking you, "What do you want us to decide?" is not the language of leaders.

As CEO, you find that with the exception of the governance responsibilities you are given, the expectations placed on you by the board are unclear. You may often be confused about what exactly the board wants. You may be equally confused, at least some of the time, about which decisions you are allowed to make and under what circumstances you can rely on the board to back you up. The effect this has on your ability to delegate to others is immense. You cannot confidently give to others the right to make decisions when you doubt that the right was yours to give away! And of course, when it is hard to discern the board's expectations, you know that the criteria used to assess your performance can be unpredictable, changeable, or even capricious.

The Board-CEO Relationship in the Policy Governance Model

In Policy Governance, the relationship between the CEO and the board of directors is of major importance. That relationship, well conceived, can set the stage for effective management. It is often said that the most important task of a board is the hiring of the chief executive. Although hiring is surely important, the establishment of an effective relationship is even more important.

The effective board relationship with an executive is one that recognizes that job products of board and executive are truly separate. Effectiveness calls for two strong, totally different responsibilities. Either party trying to do the other's job is interfering with effective operation. It is not the board's job to save you from the responsibilities of your job, nor is it your job to save the board from the responsibilities of governance.

Further, who works for whom must be clear. The board can respect, even revere, your skills, commitment, and leadership. But the board should never slip subtly into acting as if it works for you.

In Policy Governance, your job is defined by the board (acting as a body). It is to produce organizational accomplishment and conduct that can be shown to be a reasonable interpretation of board policies about ends and executive limitations. This is a major job, but it is designed by the board in such a way that you are given a great amount of discretion and decision-making authority. Accordingly, your formal relationship with the board is to receive its instructions and deliver its expectations. Informally, because you are empowered to seek advice from whomever you choose, you are likely to interact in many ways with board members. But you will not be required to treat them on an individual basis as your boss.

Your relationship to the board under Policy Governance is more clear, more predictable, and more fair. It is also much more demanding, as the removal of board-imposed advice-giving bodies and the elimination of ambiguity in your job requirements give you nowhere to hide. Organizational success (that is, the accomplishment of ends and the avoidance of off-limits means) is viewed as your having done well. Organizational failure to achieve ends or to avoid certain means is viewed as your failure. You will be held to the "any reasonable interpretation" test and will need to be able to justify your decisions according to that standard, not the standard of the individual preferences of individual board members.

We noted earlier in this CarverGuide the expectations traditionally placed on CEOs with respect to planning and running board meetings. Let's look now at your role as the Policy Governance board conducts its meetings.

Your board's meeting agenda contains only those items that relate to its job products: linkage with the ownership, explicit governing policies, and assurance of executive performance. In this way, it maintains control over the agenda. This releases you from the onerous task of having to tell your board what to do. So you will have little to put onto the agenda. Certainly you will not create the board's agenda; that is the board's job. You may be asked to bring information about policy options and their various implications. You might also make spokespersons available to the board for the different policy alternatives the board is exploring. In this manner, you will be providing help to the board as it deliberates the decisions it must make, but you will be providing the help that it asked for. Notice how closely this parallels the situation in which you as CEO are allowed to be in charge of the advice you need.

In Policy Governance, boards do not approve staff actions because the board's engagement in operational documents trivializes its job and severely hampers managerial agility. Further, because of the board's manner of delegation (do anything that works to accomplish the ends except use the means we have placed off-limits), there is nothing that you will need to have approved. So approvals vanish from the board's agenda.

Once a board has established the criteria that tell the CEO its expectations, it must then monitor to ensure that performance is in line with expectations. The board may obtain its monitoring data in any of three ways: (1) by getting it from you; (2) by getting it from an objective, disinterested outsider, like an auditor; or (3) by collecting the data itself (direct inspection). If the board is expecting you to provide the data, then you collect data that directly address the policy being monitored. Neither financial statements and balance sheets nor attendance data nor many of the usual reports that boards look at will directly monitor board criteria. In fact, reports traditionally given to the board are not monitoring reports. So don't use them as monitoring reports. The board can see them if it wishes, but such reports fail to directly address policy criteria and hence provide only incidental information. Monitoring reports should allow the board to tell at a glance if the criteria in the policies are being met. It is your responsibility to produce data that enable a majority of the board to feel reasonably assured of performance.

If the board selects an outside auditor to monitor a given policy, the auditor will need to measure staff compliance with respect to a specific policy. It is important that the external party assess performance only against the board's policy. Your only role is to cooperate with the board-appointed external monitor.

If the board decides to use direct inspection as its method of monitoring a given policy, this may require an on-site visit or inspection of staff documents. It is important for the board to realize that this monitoring method should not be used unless the board role and discipline are in excellent order, lest it deteriorate into meddling. Your responsibility is simply to cooperate.

The board and its chief executive constitute a leadership team. Their contributions are formally separable, and once clearly differentiated, the two roles can be supportive and respectful of each other. As in sports, the team functions only so long as the positions are clearly defined at the outset.

The foremost expectation of mutual support is that each function remain true to its particular responsibility. You must be able to rely on the board to confront and resolve issues of governance while respectfully staying out of management. The board must be able to rely on you to confront and resolve issues of management while respectfully staying out of governance.

The board has the right to expect performance, honesty, and straightforwardness in its CEO. Boards can at times be understanding about performance but should never bend an inch on integrity. You have the right to expect the board to be clear about the rules and then to play by them. You have the right to expect the board to speak with one voice despite the diverse opinions that can be found within the board's constituencies. And you have the right to expect the board to get its own job done.

The Importance of Trust in the Board-CEO Relationship

We have talked in general about the relationship between yourself and your board. Now we want to focus on the issue of trust. How healthy is the trust between your board and yourself? While we all know that things work better when such trust exists and that things become unpleasant and inefficient when it doesn't, we are not sure about how to restore that trust once it slips away—or indeed how to establish it meaningfully in the first place.

Trust is always an issue. Any board needs to trust its CEO to give honest information and to carry out its directives. Any CEO needs to trust the board to be fair in judgment and never capricious in action.

Under conditions of mistrust, the human toll is high. Board members and CEOs alike become unhappy. Boards worry that they are accountable for an organization that may be malfunctioning, and their ability to govern becomes hampered when they cannot rely on management's information or good will. CEOs feel hesitant about carrying out their jobs, fearing unfair judgment.

In our experience, however, most instances of lack of trust between board and CEO arise for reasons unrelated to personal integrity. Boards and CEOs are more frequently troubled by lack of trust that stems from poor governance than that which stems from poor character. Boards stating that they don't trust their CEOs rarely have been clear to their CEOs about their expectations. If they are clear and if they monitor compliance with their expectations, there is little mistrust to accumulate.

We have seen mislabeled trust problems resolve themselves as a board begins to follow a few simple but effective tenets of good governance. Happily, the same rules can help organizations avoid developing such problems in the first place. So even if your board is free from problems of trust now, paying attention to these tips may well be worth your effort down the line. If your board is trying to attain Policy Governance discipline:

- Urge your board to say clearly what it expects. It is quite common for boards to trust CEOs to read their minds! This trust is necessarily short-lived. Boards should put their expectations into a set of explicit policies about organizational outputs (ends) and limitations on the latitude of staff decisions and actions (executive limitations).

- Remember that only the single board voice counts. The only relevant expectations for management are those that the board has officially adopted. That means a vote has been taken. Expectations of individual board members should be of no effect and cannot be interpreted as the intent of the whole board.

- Expect that you will only be judged according to stated criteria. One of those criteria will be that you will only give honest and accurate information to the board.

It is common, when talking of trust issues between board and CEO, to address the board's ability to trust the CEO. In Policy Governance, the combination of clear expectations and careful monitoring makes trust a rather more minor issue for boards to concern themselves with. Another aspect of trust needs to be noted, however. *The CEO's ability to trust the board* is a major factor. CEOs have long been accustomed to boards checking performance against unstated and unclear criteria. They are used to boards sometimes undermining CEO authority by intruding into sub-CEO levels of organization and even by directly countermanding CEO instructions. CEOs are also accustomed to boards failing to protect them and their staff from renegade, intrusive individual board members.

CEOs know that under these circumstances, they will find ways to protect themselves against ambushes by the board, even at the expense of organizational efficiency. Policy Governance makes this unnecessary, since if the board follows the principles of the model, it will have rigorous but fair expectations and will act in a way that makes CEO trust in the fairness and predictability of the board a reasonable rather than a foolhardy step.

CEOs should therefore act with a Policy Governance board as if they believe that they truly have been given all the expectations on which their job depends. This means making the decisions the board empowers them to make, knowing they will have to bear only the test of proving that the decision was a reasonable interpretation of board policy.

Boards and CEOs that follow these general rules will find that trust problems disappear—or are prevented from forming in the first place. The time to safeguard and nourish trust is before it slips away.

Helping the Board Choose Policy Governance

Questions often asked by CEOs regarding Policy Governance are: How can I take this message back to my board? and How can I get my board to operate in this new way?

Here is your dilemma. You learn about Policy Governance in a workshop or by reading. You are convinced that the model should replace traditional modes of governing but cannot single-handedly make the switch. After all, you have no legitimate authority over the board. What do you do?

Remember that one of the tenets of Policy Governance is that the board must not default to the CEO in the determination of its job. Board policies in Policy Governance must express the board's values, not the CEO's. So you encounter a paradoxical impasse: if you spoon-feed Policy Governance to the board, it won't be Policy Governance!

While admitting that in the real-life setting there may be no easy solution to balancing these concerns, we can offer a few tips to help you carry the Policy Governance torch home.

- Return from your exposure to Policy Governance as a discoverer. Approach your board as an explorer who has found a new pass through the mountains. Embody the excitement of new knowledge rather than the pushiness of evangelical fervor. The message is more "Wow, look what I found!" than "You've got to change and go this way." Explain to your board that you've come across something that can make its job clearer and more effective.
- Emphasize board potential, not flaws. No doubt about it, boards do need to confront the defects of traditional governance. But they'll hear the message better if your focus is on opening up the tremendous potential for leadership. It is wise to emphasize the

positive. Otherwise, board members may recoil before hearing the whole story, an understandable reaction to having their methods criticized. After all, haven't some of them spent decades learning the conventional ways?

• Play student, not expert. Remember that you've just begun learning yourself, so if you try to explain more than you can substantiate you may lose credibility, doing yourself and your board a disservice.

• Pass the torch—nurture a champion. A genuine rebirth will more likely come to pass if the banner is waved by a board member rather than by the CEO. This method must be sensitively handled, for the idea is to give helpful tools to board members who truly want to increase the board's effectiveness. It is as counterproductive as it is disingenuous to manipulate a board member into fronting your own agenda.

• Arrange Policy Governance exposure. Acquaint your board with Policy Governance in a retreat or training event or through published materials. If your board already relies on you to be its source of training and development, you can use that expectation as a vehicle for returning to the board its own leadership. But be up-front about it; declare that the event will challenge traditional ideas, including those held by board members and, yes, by you too.

• Work with the chair. Through discussions or sharing materials, help your chair see that governance could be much improved, even though your board may be the world's best in using traditional governance. Most conscientious chairs will take to the idea of leaving a legacy of superior governance. If approached in this way, the best possible champion, the chair, might lead the way.

• Turn off the trivia tap. To the extent that you can legitimately and safely do so, stop the commonplace practice of bringing your board endless trivia. Be sure your staff stops, too. Somehow staff members have come to think it is their responsibility to keep board members involved, so they involve them in staff decisions. Staffs have been teaching the wrong lessons for a long time.

• Focus reports and remarks on underlying values. Use the ends-means distinction to focus even traditional reporting on the underlying values that make a difference. For example, if you are presenting a budget to a tradition-bound board, highlight the major budget values instead of the myriad individual numbers. Help the board see that its job is not just to examine the world through your documents but to operate on an entirely different plane.

• Focus on the ends challenge. Continually bring board deliberations back to a discussion of ends. What results are we seeking? Why those results instead of all the other possible results the world needs? Are we being ambitious enough? Or are our aims so unattainably high that they make better rhetoric than instruction? Why should our results be for this set of recipients rather than that one? What are we saying about the relative worth of achieving certain results for certain populations? Don't initiate discussions of programs, services, or curricula with the board; discuss the ends toward which these staff activities might be aimed.

Be very cautious in your use of the last three of the tips just given. Your Policy Governance emphasis might seem presumptuous to the board and, in fact, comes close to encroaching upon board prerogatives. We include them here because, if sensitively done, they might provide a positive influence on the board's choice of governance method.

Helping Your Board Stay on Track

If you are a CEO whose board has elected to use Policy Governance, remember first that the primary responsibility for using the model well lies with the board. Then remember: you can take actions that will make it more likely that the board stays on track. The board will be struggling to use a counterintuitive model well. There are many sources of inducement for a board to drift back into time-honored, if ineffective, ways. Don't be one of them!

Your interactions with the board should be model-consistent at all times. This means that you must avoid some traps. Here are some examples.

• Your board has defined the ends it expects the organization to accomplish and the means that the organization may not use. You have been given the right to use any reasonable interpretation of its words. Use it. Do not ask the board to further elucidate upon its policies. It defined them in as much detail as it wished. Its job is not to define until you are satisfied, but until it is satisfied.

• Do not take your plans to the board to see what it thinks. This is tantamount to asking for its approval. If the board approves of your plan, can you change it later? If it doesn't approve of your plan, and if it was a reasonable interpretation of board policies, what do the board policies and delegation method now amount to?

• If you wish to consult with individual board members about an issue (the only reason for doing this is that the individual has skill or knowledge in that area), make it clear that you are looking for input but have not forgotten that you, not the board member, will be held accountable for the decision you will eventually make.

• If your board asks for information about a decision that it is going to be making (Policy Governance boards often seek input from CEOs and staff as well as many other parties about their decisions), provide unbiased, accurate information about the options the board has. Tell the board what you see as the implications of the various options. Clearly mark the report as unrelated to your compliance with established policies. That is, it is not a monitoring report.

• If your board has requested monitoring data on a policy from you (Policy Governance boards get much, though not all, of their monitoring data from the CEO), give the board only the data that directly address the policy being monitored. Extra information, though interesting, is not monitoring data and should not be confused with it. Make sure that the data truly do address policy criteria. If the board wants certain consumers to know how to swim, telling it how many people went to swimming class does not answer the question.

• If the board has stated that it expects you to keep it informed on matters about which it has set no criteria, and about which it is not making decisions (incidental information), give it this sort of information in a format that clearly marks it as information that is not monitoring information.

• Never allow decision, monitoring, and incidental information from you to the board to get mixed up.

Summary

In this CarverGuide, we have covered your role as a CEO, what your overall relationship with your board should be, and how you can support your board's governance without intruding into it.

You must learn to be your board's best booster, yet not interfere with the board's being responsible for itself. Your commendable sense of responsibility for making everything come out right for the organization can easily extend even to areas where you have no legitimate authority. Don't let it. You must get beyond thinking that you are more responsible than the board is for the board's being responsible. In the long run, board members' taking responsibility for board effectiveness is the only path to governance integrity and the only foundation for a superior board-CEO relationship.

The CarverGuide
Series on Effective
Board Governance

The Policy Governance model was created by John Carver in the mid 1970s as a radical alternative to the conventional wisdom about how governance should proceed. All governance literature at that time—as virtually all of it is even today—was based on ideas about the board's role and responsibilities that had been around for a very long time.

Boards convinced that Policy Governance offers a breakthrough in governance thinking encounter a confusing problem: most printed matter and training reinforce old governance ideas rather than the new ones. It is not that widely available sources do not have wisdom to offer. Indeed, they do. But the wisdom they have is rooted in traditional governance ideas. One of the great difficulties of a paradigm shift is that perfectly fine wisdom in a previous paradigm can become poor judgment in a new one. The person most expert in flying a propeller-driven plane is not, therefore, expert in piloting a jet.

Consequently, most current guides and training materials can actually handicap boards trying to use the new governance ideas in Policy Governance. The CarverGuide series was created to remedy this situation. The series offers detailed guidance on specific board responsibilities and operations based on the *new* paradigm rather than the traditional approach.

The first CarverGuide in the series presented an overview of the fundamental principles of the Policy Governance model. As a model, Policy Governance is designed to embrace all further issues of governance that are specific to different organizations and different circumstances. That is, it is not specifically about fiscal oversight, CEO evaluation, planning, agenda control, committee operation, or the other many facets of board leadership. It is, in fact, about all of them. It is a basic set of concepts and principles that lay the groundwork for determining appropriate board leadership about these and other common governance issues. Nonetheless, many boards need specific materials that individually do address these different facets of board leadership.

Having presented the overview in the first CarverGuide, we deal with the various areas of board concern one at a time in the succeeding guides in this series. It is our hope that the concepts and recommendations we present in this series will help all boards achieve a powerful overhaul of their approach to governance. Indeed, the practices we recommend in the CarverGuide Series really make sense only as parts of the larger picture of board leadership held up by the Policy Governance model.